Who's a Clever Boy, Then?

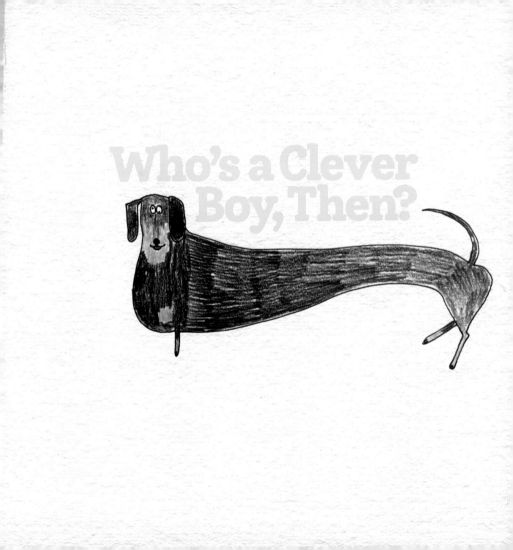

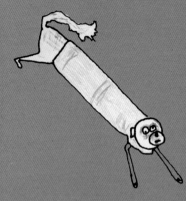

For our dog, Narla

Who's a Clever Boy, Then?

Hercule Van Wolfwinkle

HarperCollins*Publishers*

HarperCollins*Publishers*
1 London Bridge Street
London SE1 9GF

www.harpercollins.co.uk

HarperCollins*Publishers*
1st Floor, Watermarque Building, Ringsend Road
Dublin 4, Ireland

First published by HarperCollins*Publishers* 2022

10 9 8 7 6 5 4 3 2 1

Text and illustrations
© Hercule Van Wolfwinkle 2022

Hercule Van Wolfwinkle asserts the moral right
to be identified as the author of this work

A catalogue record of this book is available
from the British Library

ISBN 978-0-00-854517-8

Designed by Bobby Birchall, Bobby&Co, London
Printed and bound in Latvia

MIX
Paper from
responsible sources
FSC™ C007454

FSC
www.fsc.org

This book is produced from independently
certified FSC™ paper to ensure responsible
forest management.

For more information visit:
www.harpercollins.co.uk/green

Contents

WARNING: THIS BOOK MAY CONTAIN
UNVERIFIED 'FACTS' FROM WAYWARD CATS.

Foreword

'Hercule Van Wolfwinkle' and 'art' were four words never uttered in the same sentence before one fateful day in 2020 when he doodled a picture of their family dog. The picture was rubbish, so naturally he stuck it on Facebook, jokingly offering pet portraits for sale at a modest sum of £299. No VAT.

His self-proclaimed 'ultra-realistic' illustration style is akin to that of a small child who has never seen an animal before and is only just learning how to hold a pencil properly. But, to Hercule's great surprise, people embraced the little talent he had!

What followed was a whirlwind rise to worldwide fame and an ever-increasing gaggle of disgruntled customers trying to get their hands on him.

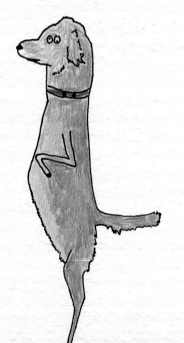

Hercule has now drawn over 1,000 pet portraits (with a waiting list of over 25,000), amassed a social media following greater than the population of High Wycombe, and raised over £150,000 and counting for two homelessness charities close to his heart, Turning Tides and Street Vet.

In this book, Hercule looks into the wonderful world of dogs, exploring some of the bizarre behaviours of our beloved four-legged friends; like, what are they thinking when they're being stroked? Why do they sometimes give us evils? And are all breeds of spaniel really banned from B&Q?

'Hercule Van Wolfwinkle' and 'art' were four words never uttered in the same sentence not all that long ago. Now they're found in the same sentence regularly – we just can't print the other words!

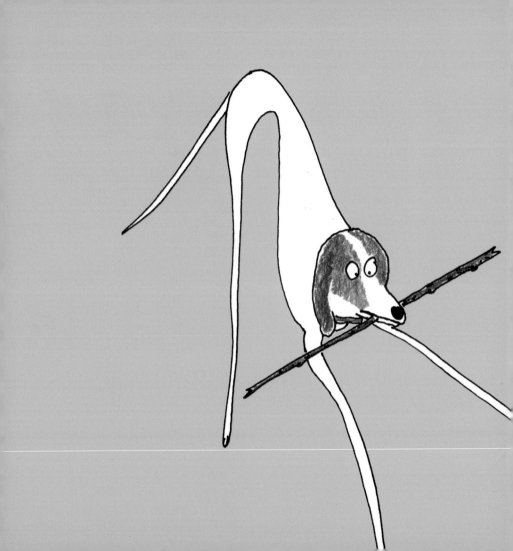

Going Walkies

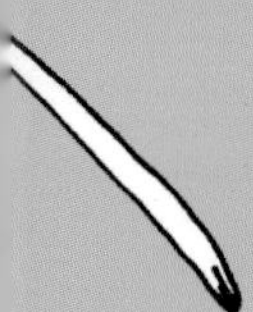

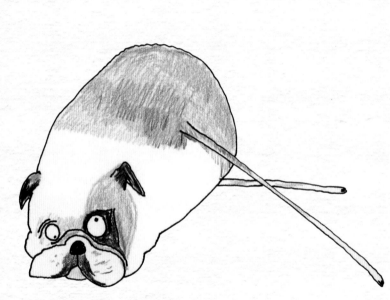

'You can say it as excitedly as you like,
I don't want to go "walkies"...'

'It might look stupid, but you wouldn't walk through puddles on all fours if your nipples got wet!'

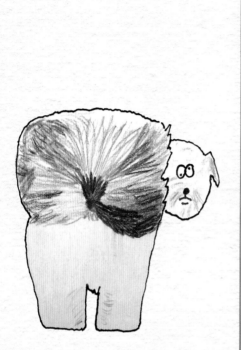

'You've come running
all the way over here
– are we going to say
hello properly or not?'

CAT FACT: 'Did you know that all spaniels are banned from B&Q after an incident in 1998 involving a Cavalier King Charles and a ballcock?'

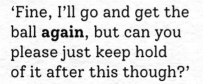

'Fine, I'll go and get the ball **again**, but can you please just keep hold of it after this though?'

'You seem to have thrown your stick away. Hang on! I'll go and find you another one ...'

'This is the best stick ever. I want you to see it, but you cannot have it.'

'I literally couldn't look more
old and grumpy if I tried.
And yet still you come,
with your ideas of play.'

'Here comes my mum now. She'll be coming to apologise to your mum because I just came charging over to you.'

'What did I tell you? Standing on a windy beach is just like sticking your head out of the car window. But without the travel sickness or flies.'

Recall Lesson No. 1

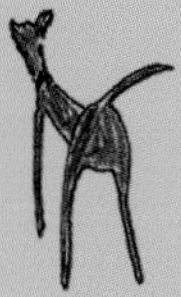

Recall Lesson No. 2

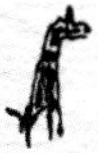

Recall Lesson No. 3

-
  Recall Lesson No. 4

Recall Training Complete.

'Oh God, she's
getting the jogging
leads ... I'm out
of here ...'

'Hang on, I'll be with you in a
minute. Just got about 94 more
blades of grass to sniff ...'

'Is that your human shouting for you?'

'Yeah.'

'Are you going to go back over to them?'

'Na, they don't sound panicked enough yet, I'll give it a little longer ...'

26

CAT FACT: 'Did you know that if a dog reaches speeds of 15 mph or more whilst running, their privates clack together?'

'I know it's only been three minutes since I last bugged you about it, but are you ready for walkies now?'

27

'Throw the ball ...
throw the ball ... no,
don't pretend to
throw the ball, JUST
THROW THE BALL!'

'I run ahead on walks
to make sure there's
no danger, but I always
wait for you to catch up.
Unless I see a squirrel.
Then you're on ya own!'

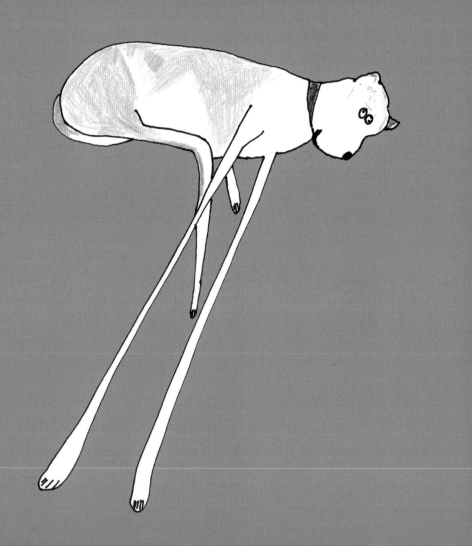

Getting
Snuggles

'I've been in love
four times in my life.

Each time with a
draught excluder.'

The number of
legs a dog grows
when it jumps
onto the sofa
with you.

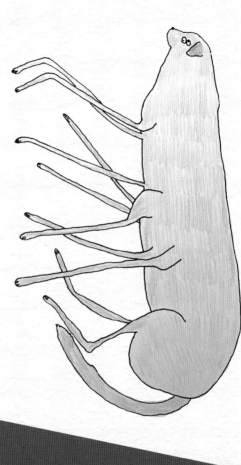

'And after I've finished inadequately cleaning myself, I'll go and put muddy paw prints all over the sofa and will probably lick the human's face with my arse tongue. And do you know what? They'll still love me.'

CAT FACT: 'Did you know that one in four dogs actually like cats? The other three just haven't got to know one.'

'Just think, one day I might get too big for cuddles like this.'

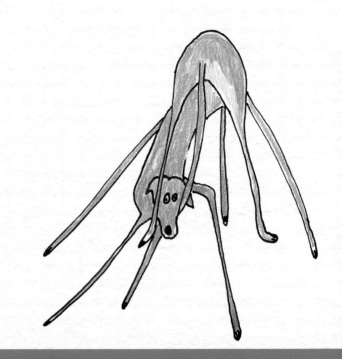

'And now I'm finally comfortable, I'll probably just nap for a couple of hours ...'

'Put that phone down, Sharon, and I'll give you more likes than Facebook ever can.'

'I'm going to enjoy this for as long as possible because you've just walked through the door and haven't seen what I've done in the kitchen yet ...'

'I'll probably start my plans to take over the world tomorrow. Or maybe the next day. Or maybe after the weekend. The next bank holiday weekend.'

'I've made a list of everything I'm going to do today. I know there's nothing on it – I never said it was a long list.'

'How's your day been?
Come sit and tell me all
about it. I'm not in the
slightest bit interested,
by the way, but it'll warm
up the seat that I'll move
to the minute you get up.'

CAT FACT: 'Did you know that the amount of oxytocin a dog produces when stroked is enough to make two lawyers agree to disagree?'

'I'm not lazy, I just like to conserve my energy for things that I know won't happen.'

'You've got your best dress on – are you going out? Here, let me cover you in slobber and hair so you have something to remember me by whilst we're apart ...'

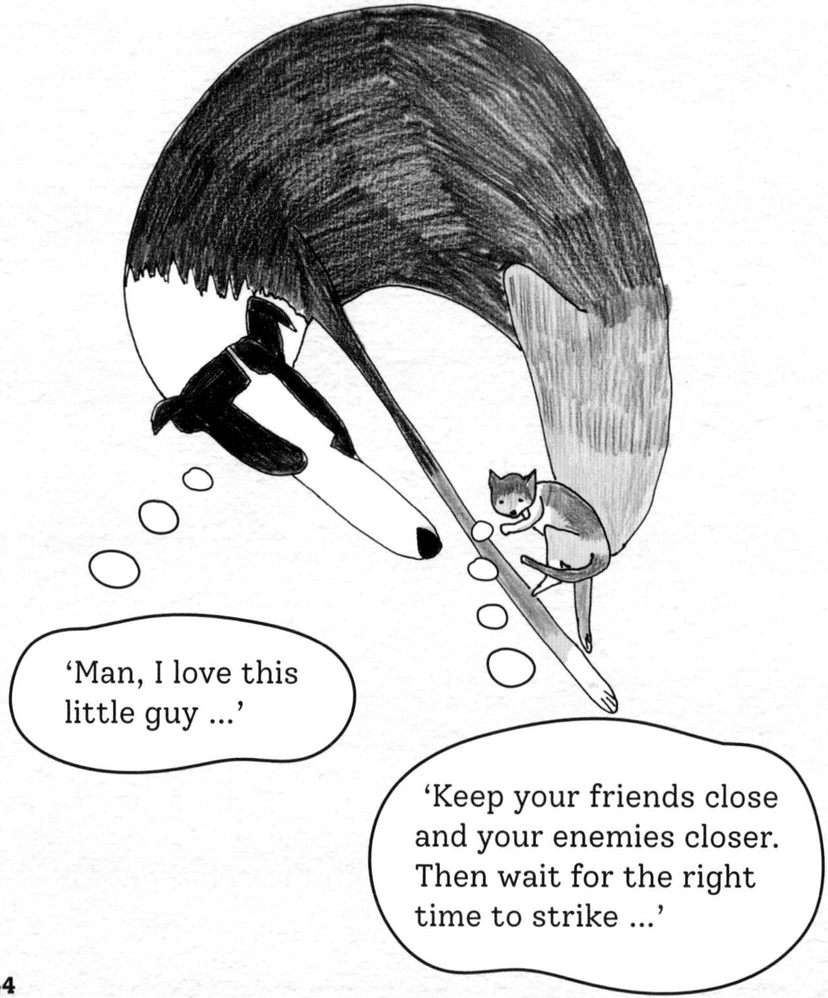
'Man, I love this little guy ...'
'Keep your friends close and your enemies closer. Then wait for the right time to strike ...'

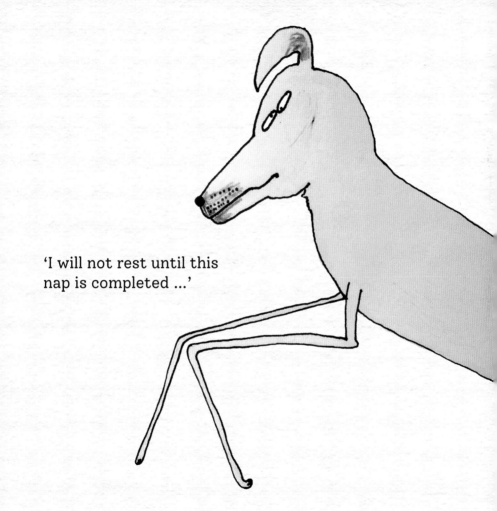

'I will not rest until this nap is completed ...'

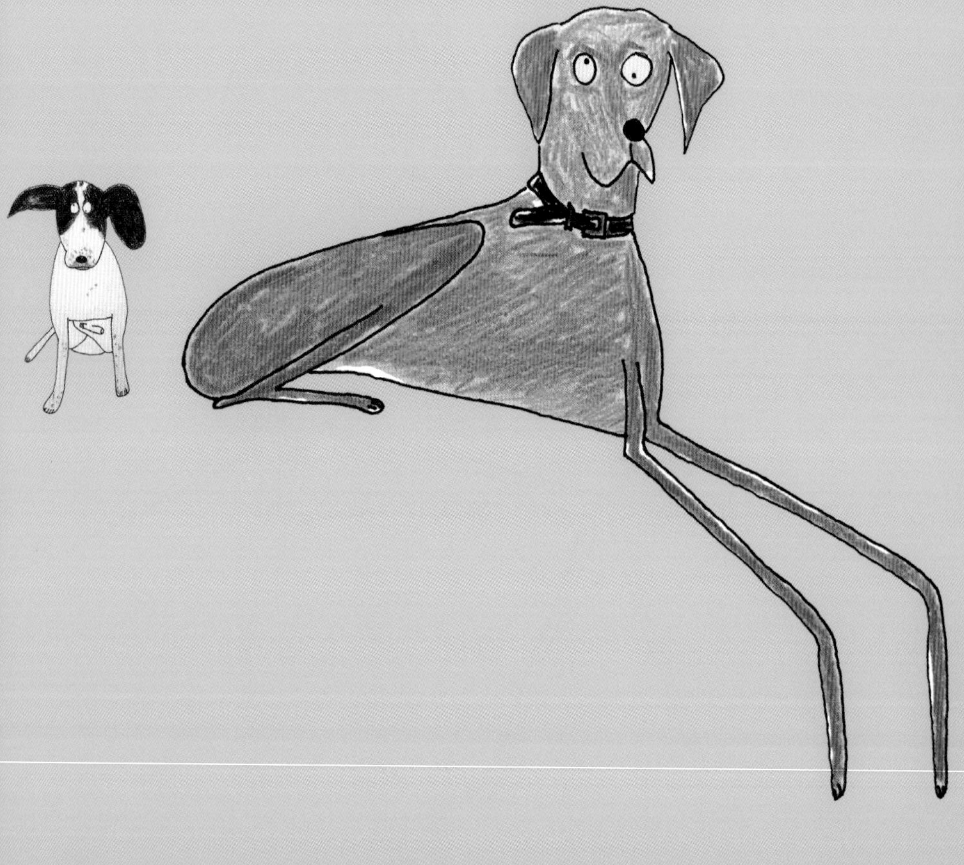

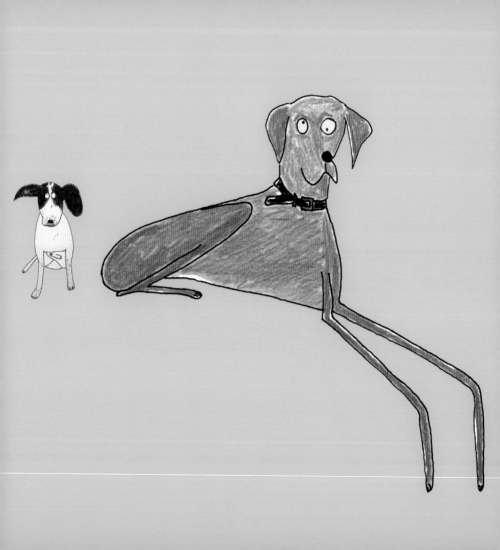

Living with Hoomans

'... and then, when they've finished, they put this big cone thing on your head which means you don't even find out what's missing for a couple of days ...'

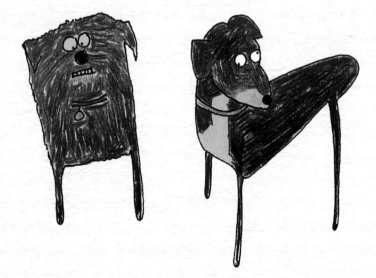

'And then we just casually wait by the door like this until they get the hint ...'

'And we just stay like this until they finish talking.'

'Then what?'

'Then hopefully she throws the ball again ...'

'And how
long do they
talk for?'

'Sometimes
ages ...'

'I'm not saying it's definitely time
to get the hoover out, Kev, but
I'm picking up fluff in places I
don't want to pick up fluff ...'

CAT FACT: 'Did you know that not all German shepherds are either German or shepherds? I know one who is a security guard from Crawley.'

'And sometimes I can do this stretch without even blowing off. Unlike you at yoga.'

'I'll be honest, I've got no idea what you're saying. But if I tilt my head like this, it at least looks like I'm trying to understand.'

'Can I have some privacy, please? Do I watch you when you're washing yourself? Well, yes, OK, I do when you leave the bathroom door open ...'

55

'... and since they've been working from home, I never get a moment's peace. There are constant trips to the kitchen getting snacks and you know I can't ignore that. I'm losing at least four hours' sleep a day ...'

'They're talking about getting a new rug and, I'll be honest, I was a bit put out by that. I think I make a lovely rug when I'm lying down.'

'Oh God, you were taking pictures of me sleeping again, weren't you? You'd better not be putting them on the internet ...'

'They talk a lot.
But there's only
three words you
really need to worry
about: "breakfast",
"dinner" and "walkies".'

'You can also respond to other words if you wish – words like "sit", "stay" and "come" will usually get you extra treats at your age.'

'I know I destroyed your last book, but that doesn't mean you have to keep such a close eye on this one. Please put it down and come play ...'

'This whole you "working from home" thing isn't really working out for me so I'm going to get an office job. Interview is in an hour; how do I look?'

'I really don't think
this is my colour.'

'Which colour?'

'All of them.'

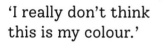

'I don't "jump up" when you're making my breakfast, I'm just trying to get as far away from those things as possible.

You could at least put some slippers on ... oh yeah, sorry, we can't mention the slippers anymore ...'

CAT FACT: 'Did you know that if a police dog farts while you're being arrested, they legally have to let you off without charge?'

'Look! Someone who doesn't like dogs – let's go charging over to them for a laugh ...'

'Shall we jump up at her too?'

'Sure, we haven't done that in ages!'

'I don't trust those cars that drive past. I don't trust that dog who lives opposite. I don't trust that couple who walk by. I don't trust them birds. I don't trust that person who puts letters through our door. And I definitely don't trust next door's cat who sits on the front wall. It's a good job I'm here to keep an eye on them all ...'

'I like to think I'm quite good at sensing human emotions, but I don't think I'll ever stop jumping out of my skin every time they leap off the sofa shouting "Goal!".'

'You said if the
dog does a poo
I need to pick it up ...
now what?'

Rover had resorted to some extreme measures to avoid being taken to the grandchildren's house.

'I'm sorry to interrupt the most important part of the film you're watching, but I've decided that now is the optimal time for someone to have to let me outside to pee.'

'What have I learnt during my time as the office dog? People like me more than they like the photocopier. People like Fridays more than they like me. People hate Mondays more than anything.'

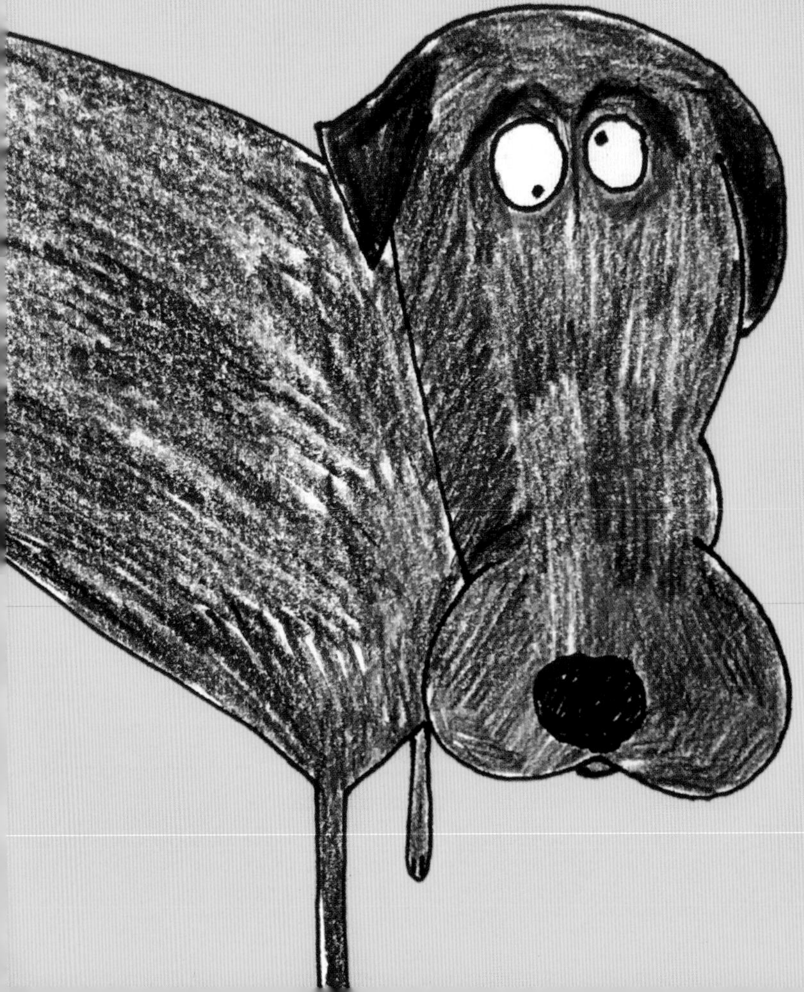

Hungry

'Did someone say "cheese"? Food kind or photo kind? No worries either way – I like both!'

'I don't even know I'm doing it; it just comes out when I'm concentrating. And right now, I'm concentrating on those crisps you're eating ...'

'This is my "creeping to the fridge in the night" walk.'

'And this, this is my "creeping back from the fridge in the night" walk.'

'Look cute and she might give
us some of those crisps ...'
'Gottle o' geer ... gottle o' geer ...'

'The handshake makes it legally binding; you now owe me a biscuit.'

'I'm 99 per cent sure it's not dinner time yet, but that sounded like rustling from the kitchen ... I should probably go and check ...'

'We will stay like this
the whole time you're
eating. Watching.
Waiting. Hoping.'

'And IIIIIIIIIIIIIIIIIIIIII
will always love
fooooooooood.'

'I've recently started a successful rehoming programme for abandoned biscuits.'

'He doesn't rehome them, he eats them.'

'I didn't say where I rehome them.'

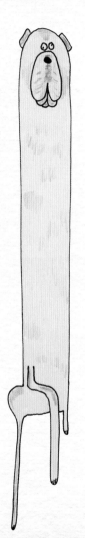

'Someone new has arrived home – let "Operation pretend the dog hasn't been fed yet" commence ...'

CAT FACT: 'Did you know that if you hold a seashell up to a Labrador's ear, they hear the sound of a packet of crisps being opened?'

'I won't be eating one of those black and yellow garden sweets again.'

'If they think I'm wearing
that, they've got another
thing coming ...'

'Treats! They always
get me with the treats!'

'Is that my dinner
you're getting ready?
Let's see ...'

'... hang on, you're
measuring it!
Why are you
measuring it?
You don't measure
your own food!'

'I'm doing the eyes at Mummy so she will think we've been neglected by Daddy and we'll get second breakfast.'

'Ooooh, second breakfast! My favourite meal of the day.'

Looking Good

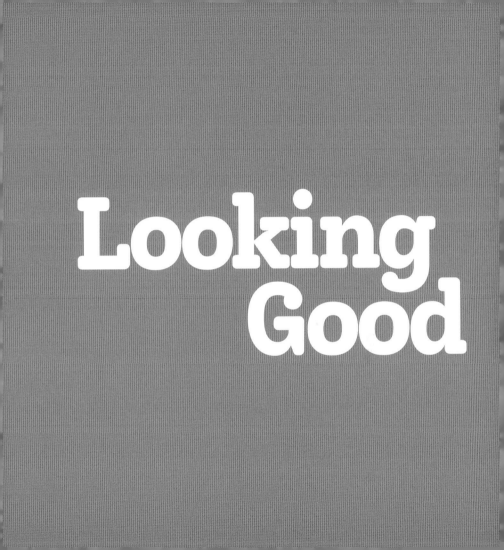

'It's a bit tight. Does it look a bit tight? Can't we just agree not to go for walks when it's wet? I mean, the rain does nothing for my hair anyway.'

'We've had to stop using the retractable lead on a windy day. One big gust and I was 30 feet in the air like a wayward kite.'

'Sure, put a silly hat on me and laugh away. Just know this: later today you'll be picking up my sh*t with a bag that can, at best, be described as "adequate" for the job in hand. And that's why I'll be making eye contact with you the whole time I'm producing it.'

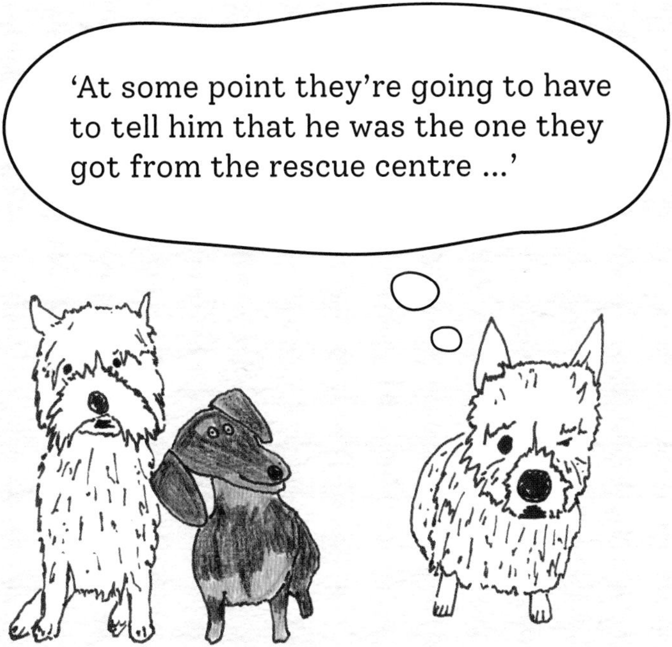
'At some point they're going to have to tell him that he was the one they got from the rescue centre ...'

'She saw one
Chihuahua in a Gucci
bag on Instagram
and now I get carried
everywhere like this!'

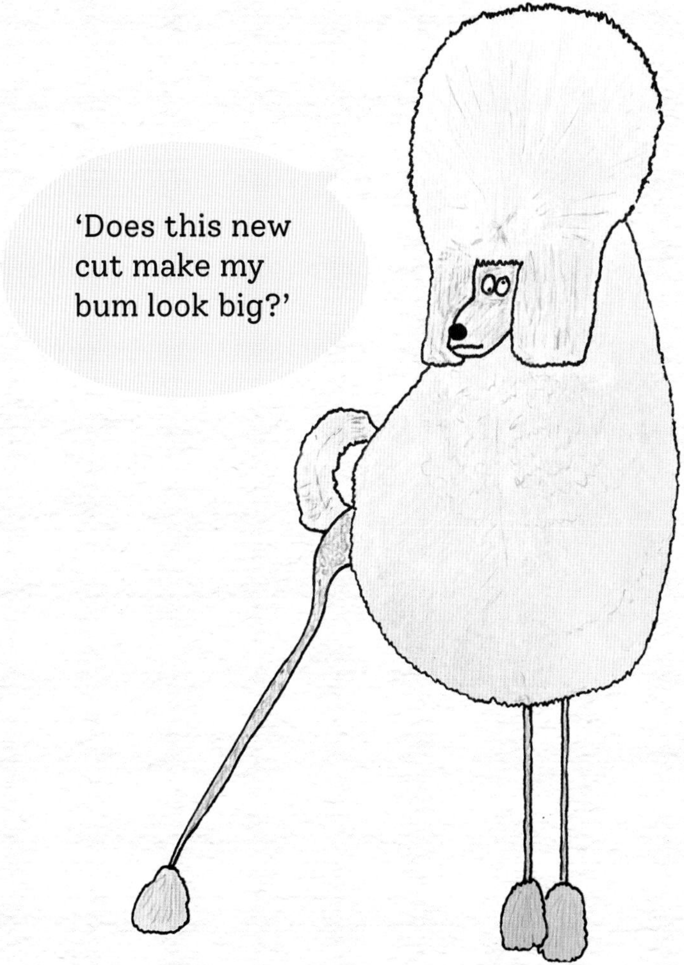
'Does this new cut make my bum look big?'

CAT FACT: 'Did you know that when you shave a Dalmatian, there's a 78 per cent chance that you will miss a spot?'

'... and I can get away with paying guinea pig prices on the bus, which is so much cheaper ...'

Expectations of trip
to the groomers ...

... vs reality of trip
to the groomers.

'I'm going to level with you: I don't think this is what the vet had in mind when she asked if you had a cone at home.'

'What do you mean
I can't go out dressed
like this?! I saw a
pug on Instagram
yesterday wearing
a leather jacket!'

'Yep, definitely
not pissing on that
humming fence
ever again ...'

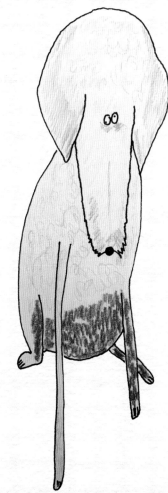

'Now can we go to the groomers? I've been wanting to change this style for weeks!'

'You know if you take me out wearing those, I'm going to pull on the lead to get as far away from you as possible. You're so embarrassing sometimes.'

'Why do you put all that stuff on your face? I think you're beautiful just as you are. Let me help you take it off!'

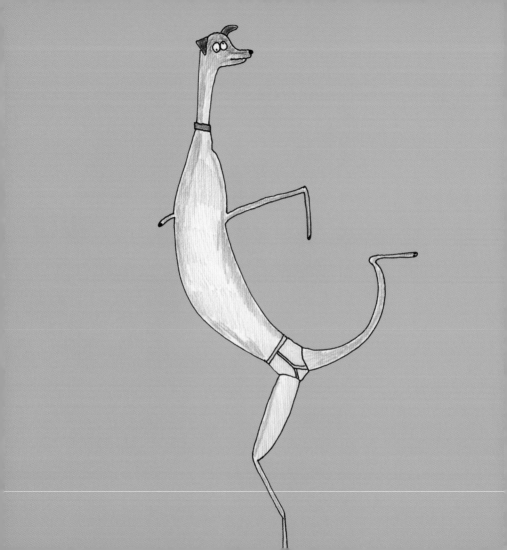

Up to Mischief

Never underestimate ...

... the courage, stubbornness
or stupidity of a dog.

Did you know that when a sophisticated dog scooches across a carpet on its arse, it can tell you the thread count, depth of pile and country in which it was manufactured?

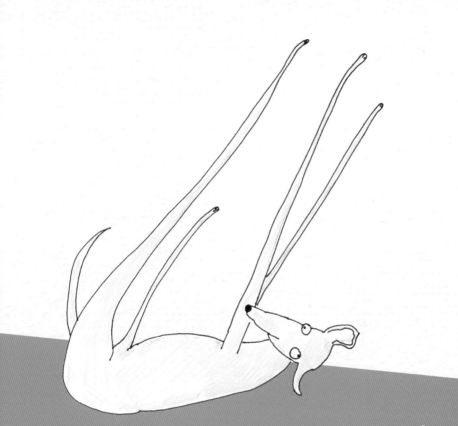

'Don't worry, it's not fox poo. OK, I lied, it is fox poo. I just can't resist it!'

111

'How do you expect us to be effective
guard dogs when we can barely see out
the window? Tell you what, we'll just
protect you by destroying anything
that person in the red coat puts
through the door each morning ...'

'The end of another busy and successful day of keeping next door's cat out of the garden ...'

CAT FACT: 'Did you know that when left at home alone, Dobermans will often perform scenes from the hit musical *Cats*?'

'Yep, that was me. Being honest, there are times when I feel lucky to be able to get my nose this far away from my arse.'

'He loved his job as a sniffer dog, but he was never the same after that time he actually found some drugs.'

'OMD! OH MY DOG!
THERE'S SOMEONE
AT THE DOOR!'

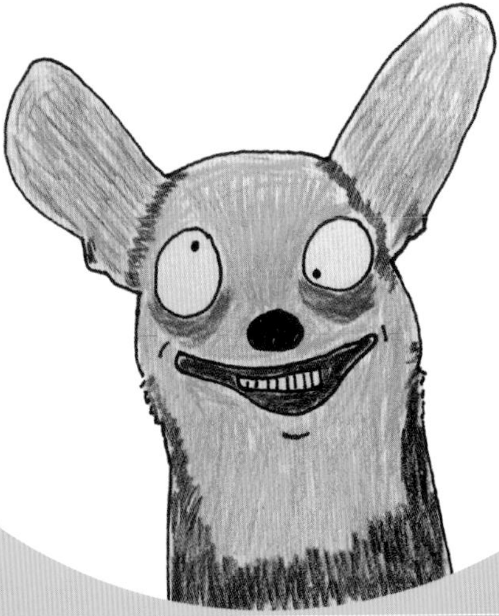

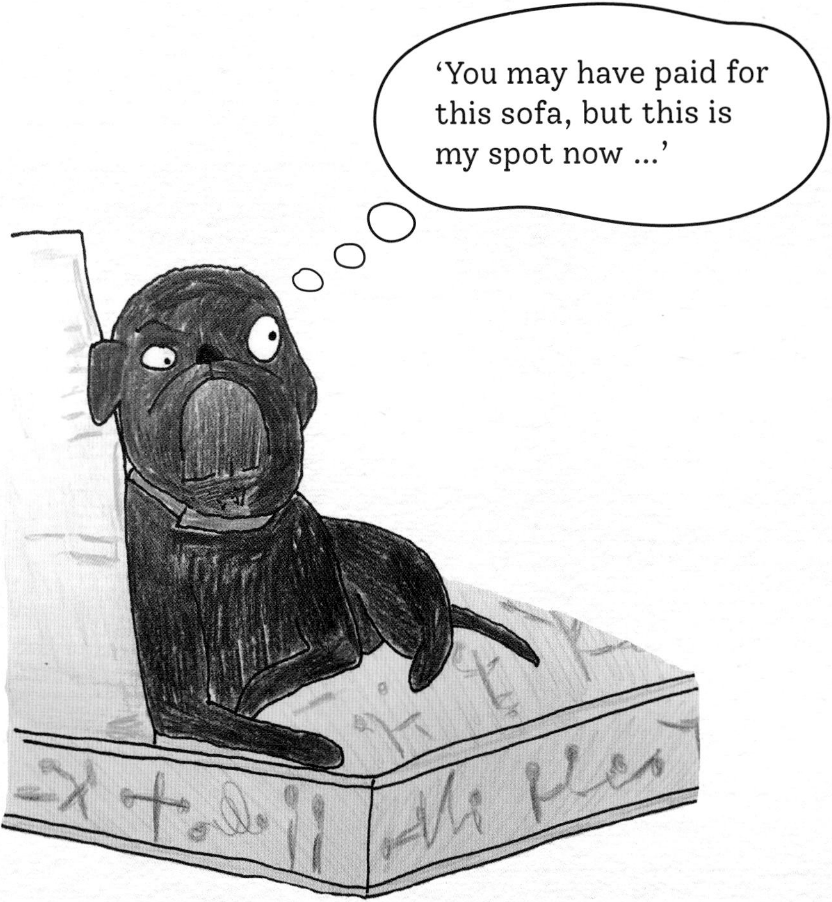
'You may have paid for this sofa, but this is my spot now ...'

'You off to work?
Cool, have fun.
I'll be here when
you get back.
Probably won't move.'

'Ha! She's seen the shoes.
She's definitely seen
the shoes. You are in so
much trouble ...'

'Where are you going? The shop? Oh phew, that should only be five minutes. Hurry back!'

'That was the longest five
minutes of my liiiiiiiiife.
I didn't think you were ever
coming back; I lost my mind.
I even collected up all my
hair off the floor and made
myself a friend.'

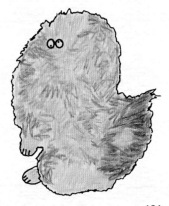

'You don't cover up the sound of a blow-off by making the sound of a fake blow-off! Bark ... cough ... sneeze ... something like that.'

'Why not? It's a double bluff.'

'Double guff more like.'

CAT FACT: 'Did you know that when a dog goes out to the garden and barks, they are telling the whole neighbourhood your secrets? DO. NOT. TRUST. YOUR. DOG. WITH. SECRETS!'

'I'm so glad you're home! But I hope you don't need a poo because I've eaten all the toilet paper.'

'It's not "incessant barking", it's just sometimes difficult to make yourself heard from down here.'

'Can you give me
some treats so that
I can go bury them
and fill in all those
holes I've dug in
the garden?'

'Sometimes the world is just a little better when it's upside down.'

'Is that the car door?
Oh God, they're home.
Look how clean and tidy
the place is; they're going
to wonder what I've been
up to all morning ... quick,
chew the newspaper up
or something!'

127

'I can't even remember
why I came into this room …
oh well, I'll just pee on the
carpet and leave; wouldn't
want a wasted trip …'